THAI VEGETARIAN COOKING

IN A NUTSHELL

THAI VEGETARIAN COOKING

A STEP-BY-STEP GUIDE

ANNE JOHNSON

ELEMENT

SHAFTESBURY, DORSET • BOSTON, MASSACHUSETTS • MELBOURNE, VICTORIA

© Element Books Limited 1999

First published in
Great Britain in 1999 by
ELEMENT BOOKS LIMITED
Shaftesbury, Dorset SP7 8BP

Published in the USA in 1999 by
ELEMENT BOOKS INC
160 North Washington Street, Boston
MA 02114

Published in Australia in 1999 by
ELEMENT BOOKS LIMITED
and distributed by Penguin Australia Ltd
487 Maroondah Highway, Ringwood,
Victoria 3134

All rights reserved.
No part of this book may be reproduced or
utilized in any form or by any means,
electronic or mechanical, without prior
permission in writing from the publisher.

Anne Johnson has asserted her right
under the Copyright, Designs and Patents
Act, 1988, to be identified as Author of
this Work.

NOTE FROM THE PUBLISHER
Unless specified otherwise
All recipes serve four
All eggs are medium
All herbs are fresh
All spoon measurements are level
Tablespoon = 15ml spoon
Teaspoon = 5ml spoon
Both metric and Imperial
measurements have been given. To
ensure success, when making a recipe,
follow one set of measurements only;
do not mix them.

Designed and created with Element Books
by The Bridgewater Book Company Ltd.

ELEMENT BOOKS LIMITED
Managing Editor Miranda Spicer
Senior Commissioning Editor Caro Ness
Editor Finny Fox-Davies
Group Production Director Clare Armstrong
Production Controller Claire Legg

THE BRIDGEWATER BOOK
COMPANY
Art Director Terry Jeavons
Design and page layout by Axis Design
Editor Jo Wells
Project Editor Caroline Earle
Photography David Jordan
Home Economy Judy Williams
Picture Research Caroline Thomas

Printed and bound in Portugal by
Printer Portuguesa.

British Library Cataloguing in Publication
data available

ISBN 1 86204 544 5

*The publishers wish to thank the following for
the use of pictures:* A–Z Botanical: p.16T.
The Image Bank: pp.6B, 7T. Tony Stone
Images pp.8T, 10T, 20.

Contents

Thai vegetarian food

THE VARIETY OF VEGETABLES *available to Thai cooks is vast, including all manner of greens, aubergines, chillies, onions, spring onions, carrots, green beans, broccoli and potatoes.*

There can be few better places than Thailand to be vegetarian. The tropical monsoon climate produces an amazing abundance of fruit and vegetables, which are mainly grown organically on smallholdings. Most of the farming is done by hand, in the traditional fashion, and transported to the market straight from the fields each day. The produce may not look quite as perfect as its supermarket counterpart, but the flavour and freshness are incomparable.

Most Thais do consume fish and meat, but usually in small quantities. Meat is relatively

BELOW **A small-holding in Chang Mai Territory, Thailand.**

expensive and used less often in everyday cooking than it is in the West. With increasing tourism and Western cultural influences vegetarianism is beginning to catch on, although some Thai vegetarians still incorporate the fish sauce that is so popular in Thai cooking, in their vegetable dishes.

The Thai emphasis on fresh fruit and vegetables ensures a good supply of vitamins and minerals, which are the cornerstones of health.

Many Thai dishes are cooked very quickly, which helps to retain the nutrients in

ABOVE *Noodles are a staple part of the traditional Thai diet.*

vegetables. Steaming is another popular cooking method and this, too, conserves vitamins. The regular Thai intake of rice and noodles provides adequate supplies of carbohydrate, which should account for between 50 and 55 per cent of the daily food intake, and are therefore the body's main source of energy.

Thai vegetarian food is also low in fat and contains no dairy products (milk, yogurt, butter, cream and cheese) or their associated animal fats.

Thai cooking

THAI COOKING IS NOT DIFFICULT, *but it is a rapid process which necessitates good organization and working quickly.*

Thai cooking is quite labour-intensive because of the number of vegetables that are used, which need to be peeled, chopped or sliced. It is easier to have all the necessary ingredients prepared and laid out in small bowls or on plates before the cooking starts, ready to be added when required.

Thai kitchens are generally much simpler than those in the West, but there are a few items that are invaluable:

ABOVE *Stir-frying vegetables in a wok preserves flavour and goodness.*

- At least one chopping board.
- A range of sharp knives in various sizes or at least one very good, sharp vegetable knife. It will speed and simplify your

LEFT *A range of sharp knives and a chopping board are kitchen essentials.*

RIGHT *A cleaver is a versatile cooking tool.*

work more than any other piece of equipment.

• A heavy Chinese cleaver, which will slice easily and will also double as a garlic and chilli crusher.

• An implement for lifting, stirring and turning ingredients in a wok; Thai cooks use a cross between a ladle and a fish slice.

• A wok. Brass is traditional, but nowadays steel is more readily available and works just as well.

A wok which has one long, wooden handle is much easier to use. A large frying pan is an alternative, although a wok is preferable because it is deeper and the whole surface heats up; foods can be cooked in the central, hottest part and ingredients that are almost done can be pushed to the sides.

• A Chinese bamboo steamer or simply a colander covered with a lid or foil, and placed on a saucepan.

ABOVE *A traditional bamboo steamer is a healthy way to cook vegetables.*

• Pestle and mortar, or a coffee grinder or small blender for preparing spice mixtures.

LEFT *A steel wok with a long-handled implement for stirring and turning food.*

Healthy eating

THE KEY TO HEALTHY EATING *is to have a diet that contains balanced amounts of proteins, carbohydrates, vitamins, minerals; and fats in moderation.*

Vegetarians tend to be healthier, to live longer, be slimmer and have correspondingly lower cholesterol levels than meat eaters. They are also less likely to have bowel problems because they regularly eat plenty of fibre and complex carbohydrates. Gallstones and diverticular disease are also less likely to be a problem for vegetarians.

Protein is important for growth and the repair of bones and tissues. Although animal foods are the major sources of protein, PULSES vegetarians can consume protein in cereals, pulses, soya products and nuts. When plant foods are eaten on their own, the quality and

ABOVE **Vegetables should make up a large proportion of a healthy diet.**

value of their proteins is lower than that of animal foods (soya beans and soya products are the exceptions). However, by combining different plant sources their overall protein quality can be sufficiently raised so that it becomes on a

RIGHT **Nuts add texture, flavour and vital protein to rice.**

par with animal protein foods – for example, rice with nuts or lentils. Carbohydrates may be either simple, such as those in sucrose, or table sugar, or complex, such as those which are found in many plant foods. It is this complex form that is most beneficial because it is released slowly from foods, providing energy over a sustained period.

Fruit and vegetables provide roughage (fibre). Although

BELOW *Every diet should contain some fats and these are best taken as unsaturated fats, such as groundnut and sunflower oil.*

ABOVE *Sugar is a simple carbohydrate.*

ABOVE *Fruit is an excellent source of fibre.*

roughage does not have any nutritional or energy value, it is essential in maintaining a healthy body and is therefore a vital part of the diet. Roughage promotes the passage of waste products through the intestines and, in turn, the absorption of nutrients into the bloodstream.

Vegetable oils, such as groundnut, corn and sunflower oils, are all unsaturated fats which protect the heart. Animal fats are saturated and increase the amount of blood cholesterol which in turn increases the chances of heart disease.

Sources of nutrients

THE WAY TO GOOD HEALTH *is through eating a nutritious diet. The body needs over 50 essential nutrients (vitamins, minerals, amino acids, fatty acids) each day.*

GARLIC

Garlic has antiviral and antibacterial properties and has been used to cure many complaints, including asthma, arthritis, nasal congestion and other cold symptoms.

GARLIC

CHILLIES

Although chillies are a richer source of vitamin C than citrus fruits, because they are generally eaten in small quantities their nutritional contribution to the diet tends to be minimal.

CHOPPED CHILLIES

CAULIFLOWER

Cauliflower, like other brassicas, provides vitamins C, E and K, and flavonoids.

CAULIFLOWER

MANGETOUT

Mangetout provide vitamins B1 and C, as well as being a source of protein, fibre, folate and phosphorus.

MANGETOUT

COURGETTES

As well as providing vitamin C, courgettes are also a good source of beta-carotene and folate.

COURGETTES

GREEN BEANS

Green beans are a useful source of roughage and vitamins A, B and C.

GREEN BEANS

MUSHROOMS

Mushrooms are a good low-calorie protein source and also a useful source of potassium and other trace elements.

MUSHROOMS

LIMES

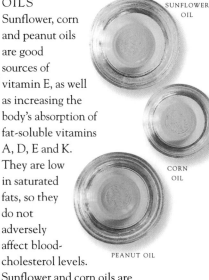

Limes, like all citrus fruits, are an excellent source of vitamin C, which is believed to

LIME SLICES maintain the strength of the immune system. Limes also contain large quantities of bioflavonoids.

BEANSPROUTS

Beansprouts are a low-calorie, rich source of vitamin C. They also contain some B vitamins.

BEANSPROUTS

RICE

Rice is a good carbohydrate source and can be eaten by those with gluten intolerance. It contains potassium and most of the B vitamins, except B12.

RICE

OILS

Sunflower, corn and peanut oils are good sources of vitamin E, as well as increasing the body's absorption of fat-soluble vitamins A, D, E and K. They are low in saturated fats, so they do not adversely affect blood-cholesterol levels.

SUNFLOWER OIL

CORN OIL

PEANUT OIL

Sunflower and corn oils are polyunsaturated fats and include the essential fatty acids that the body cannot make itself and which are necessary for cell growth and development.

TOFU

Tofu is made from soya beans. It is rich in protein, low in saturated fats and a good source of calcium and vitamin E.

TOFU

13

Herbs and spices

THAI COOKS CONSIDER A PESTLE AND MORTAR *to be essential tools for obtaining the correct texture and flavour of their spice mixtures; however, a spice grinder or a small blender can be used as an alternative.*

CORIANDER SEEDS

Coriander seeds have a fragrant lemon flavour and can be used whole, ground or roasted.

CORIANDER SEEDS

CARDAMOM

Cardamom pods can be used whole or the small black seeds can be removed. The seeds are usually toasted in a heavy, dry frying pan until they smell fragrant, then ground before use. Cardamom seeds can be chewed after a meal to cleanse the breath. They can also help to soothe the digestive system.

CARDAMOM

CHILLIES

There are many different kinds of chilli, but in general, the smaller the chilli, the hotter the flavour, and green chillies are hotter than red. Most of the heat is found in the seeds. The quantities of chillies used in this book are conservative, so if hotter dishes are preferred, increase the number of chillies and leave in the seeds.

FRESH CHILLIES

Chilli powders vary considerably in strength depending on the type of chilli used, so don't be over-generous until you have checked the flavour.

CHILLI POWDER

FRESH GINGER

Fresh root ginger is available from most supermarkets and Asian food stores. For use, ginger is usually peeled and then grated, sliced or chopped. In homeopathic medicine ginger is used to treat nausea and digestive complaints.

FRESH GINGER

GALANGAL

Galangal is a similar spice to ginger, but it has a thinner, slightly pink skin and a more mellow flavour. Galangal is prepared in the same way as ginger. It is available in good

FINELY CHOPPED GALANGAL

supermarkets and Asian food stores, either fresh or as a purée. It is also available dried, when it is known as laos powder, although fresh galangal has a better flavour than the dried form.

FRESH GALANGAL

LEMON GRASS

Lemon grass is available from good supermarkets and Asian food stores in bundles of stalks which look rather like spring onions. The coarse outer leaves should be discarded and the inner stalks thinly sliced or chopped before adding to Thai dishes. Dried and powdered lemon grass are also available, or lemon rind or juice can be substituted in recipes.

FRESH LEMON GRASS

PREPARING LEMON GRASS

1 Cut off and discard the tough outer leaves and root ends. Slice the lemon grass thinly, then chop finely.

KAFFIR LIME LEAVES

Kaffir lime leaves can be bought fresh or dried in Asian food stores and good supermarkets. Fresh leaves have a better flavour than dried leaves, and are much prized for the pungent lemony aroma that they impart to a dish. Lime or lemon rind or juice can be used instead.

KAFFIR LIME LEAVES

ABOVE *Kaffir lime is a native tree throughout Asia.*

skin, has no juice. Only the rind is used for the intense citrus flavour that it imparts to a dish.

FRESH CORIANDER

Coriander is one of the most popular herbs in Thailand. The stems, roots, leaves and seeds are all used. Fresh coriander keeps well when stored in an airtight container in the refrigerator or freezer.

FRESH CORIANDER

KAFFIR LIMES

The Oriental kaffir lime, which has darker, knobbly

KAFFIR LIMES

BASIL

Holy basil is used in Thai cookery. It has a smaller, darker leaf and is less sweet than the basil that is familiar in the West. Any basil can be used instead.

BASIL

TAMARIND

The tamarind fruit contains a dark, sticky pulp, which is available from specialist Asian and Indian food stores as a concentrated paste. Tamarind is also sold as a dried pulp that has to be soaked in water for

TAMARIND
FRUIT

several minutes, then squeezed to extract the juice. Tamarind has a slightly sour taste, which acts as a good foil to the slight sweetness of much Thai food. Lemon juice can be substituted if tamarind is not available.

MINT

Spearmint is the variety of mint that is most commonly used in Thai cooking. It is a particularly popular ingredient in salads.

1 Soak 25g (1oz) tamarind pulp in 150ml (¼ pint) warm water for 10 minutes. Squeeze out as much juice as possible.

ABOVE **A crunchy Thai salad, garnished with spearmint.**

17

Storecupboard ingredients

NOW THAT THAI FOOD *is more familiar and increasingly popular, it has become easier to find authentic ingredients in the major supermarkets, but if they are not available, these storecupboard ingredients can be bought from specialist food stores.*

RICE

The rice that is most commonly used in Thailand is fragrant or jasmine rice. This is a highly aromatic long-grain rice.

Sticky rice is a variety of short-grain rice that has a high starch content. Sticky rice is used for many Thai desserts.

BELOW *Several types of rice, noodles, palm sugar, water chestnuts, tofu, shiitake mushrooms, coconut milk, soy sauce, and bean sauces are invaluable in Thai cooking. Keep your storecupboard well stocked with a range of these basic, but essential ingredients.*

NOODLES

A variety of noodles is eaten in Thailand and each type lends its own flavour, texture and character to a dish.

Yellow egg noodles can be bought fresh or dried. Rice vermicelli are very thin and transparent and rice sticks are a wider, flatter white noodle. Very thin glass noodles, also known as cellophane or transparent noodles, are similar to rice vermicelli, but are made from mung bean flour.

FLAT RICE NOODLES

JASMINE RICE

STICKY RICE

VERMICELLI

LONG-GRAIN RICE

RICE NOODLES

DRIED EGG NOODLES

FRESH EGG NOODLES

COCONUT MILK
Coconut milk is available in cans or can be made from blocks of coconut cream, dried coconut powder or desiccated coconut.

WATER CHESTNUTS
Water chestnuts are the corms of a species of water grass. They are available fresh or canned and have a mild, slightly sweet flavour and crunchy texture.

PALM SUGAR
This type of sugar has a caramel flavour and is available in blocks. Light muscovado sugar is a suitable alternative.

TOFU
Tofu is soya bean curd, available as a 'cream' or in a firmer block that cuts and holds its shape during stir-frying.

BEAN SAUCES
Sauces made from black, yellow or red beans and available ready-made in jars.

SOY SAUCE
Soy sauce is made from fermented soya beans. Light soy sauce is paler, thinner, saltier and less sweet than dark soy sauce.

SHIITAKE MUSHROOMS
Dried shiitake mushrooms are a useful standby; they should be soaked for 15–20 minutes in hot water before use.

COCONUT MILK

SOY SAUCE

BLACK BEAN SAUCE

COCONUT MILK

PALM SUGAR   COCONUT   WATER CHESTNUTS   TOFU   SHIITAKE MUSHROOMS

Regional variations

THAILAND CAN BE DIVIDED *into four regions, each of which has its own culinary characteristics. Although Thailand is not a large country, it has a population of around 60 million people.*

The population of Thailand is varied. About forty five million are Thai, while the rest belong to several nationalities, mainly Chinese and Malay with fewer Burmese, Cambodians, Laotians and Vietnamese. With this ethnic mix, it is not surprising that Thai cooking has been influenced by other culinary traditions.

THE CENTRAL PLAINS
This is the region that supplies most of Thailand's rice. Central Thailand is dominated by the Chao Phraya River. It is a densely populated area, which includes the teeming city of Bangkok, and fertile plains

BELOW *On the central plains rice farming is common.*

where farmers tend paddy fields, fed by the many small tributaries of the Chao Phraya. The region also has abundant fruit orchards.

NORTHERN THAILAND

ABOVE *Curries betray a Burmese influence in the north.*

Garlic, shallots and chillies grow here and characterize many of the favourite northern dishes. Spices play a dominant part, too, and a vast choice of richly flavoured dishes tempt the palate. A wide choice of curries reveals a strong Burmese influence.

THE NORTH-EAST

This is an intensely fragrant area, perfumed by the heady aroma of the many herb and citrus notes that are so popular in Thai dishes. Mint, basil, coriander, kaffir limes, lemon grass and tamarind are all abundant.

MINT

SOUTHERN THAILAND AND THE ISLANDS

The south of Thailand is a paradise for those with a sweet tooth because the locally-grown palm sugar is used to make an enormous variety of sweets. They are flavoured with mild, aromatic spices, coconut and fruits, especially local pineapples. Malay and Chinese influences are also evident in the cuisine in the use of a range of spices.

BELOW *Pineapple and coconut are traditionally used as ingredients in sweets from the south.*

21

Spring Rolls

CRISP AND GOLDEN PARCELS *of tasty vegetables, this traditional recipe makes a delicious appetizer or snack.*

INGREDIENTS

3 garlic cloves, crushed

2 tbsp vegetable oil, plus extra for deep-frying

175g (6oz) carrots, coarsely grated

225g (8oz) leeks, cut into fine matchsticks

115g (4oz) mushrooms, finely sliced

6 tbsp light soy sauce

1 tsp palm sugar

1 tsp ground coriander

50g (2oz) rice vermicelli, soaked and drained

250g (9oz) spring roll wrappers, thawed if frozen

1 egg, beaten

VARIATIONS

● Use light muscovado sugar instead of palm sugar.

● Use filo pastry instead of spring roll wrappers and shallow-fry or bake.

● Use finely sliced shallots or onions instead of leeks.

1 Gently fry the garlic in the oil for 2 minutes, or until it turns golden. Add the grated carrots, chopped leeks and sliced mushrooms and fry for a further 3 minutes.

2 Stir in the soy sauce, palm sugar, ground coriander and vermicelli and continue to fry for 3 minutes.

3 Cover the wrappers with a tea towel to keep them moist. Fill one at a time. Put a little filling in one corner.

5 Deep-fry the spring rolls in batches in hot oil for 3–4 minutes, or until golden brown on all sides and crisp. Drain on kitchen paper.

4 Fold the wrapper over the filling and roll it up diagonally towards the opposite corner, pushing the sides in as you work to form a tube. Seal with beaten egg.

COOK'S TIP

Spring roll wrappers are available from specialist food stores and some supermarkets.

Sweetcorn Patties

THESE ARE ONE OF THE FAVOURITE *snacks in Thailand and sold from stalls on many street corners.*

INGREDIENTS

250g (9oz) fresh or frozen sweetcorn

4 shallots, finely chopped

1–2 fresh red chillies, seeded and chopped

2 garlic cloves, chopped

3 tbsp rice flour

4 kaffir lime leaves, shredded

salt

1 egg

vegetable oil, for frying

lime wedges, to serve

1 Place all the ingredients, except the vegetable oil and lime wedges, in a blender or food processor and process to form a coarse paste.

RED CHILLIES

VARIATION

● Use 1 teaspoon ground chilli instead of fresh chillies.

● Use plain flour instead of rice flour.

● Use canned sweetcorn instead of frozen or fresh.

KAFFIR LIME LEAVES

2 Form the paste into balls about 2.5cm in diameter. Place in a large frying pan with hot vegetable oil and flatten out each ball with a fork.

3 Fry in batches for about 3 minutes on each side, or until golden and crisp. Drain on paper towels and serve hot or cold with lime wedges.

Filled Omelettes

FILLED OMELETTES, *such as these, are sold as street food, but they can also be served as part of a main meal.*

INGREDIENTS

4 tbsp desiccated coconut

1 tbsp palm sugar

vegetable oil, for frying

8 eggs

250ml (8fl oz) coconut milk

175g (6oz) beansprouts

75g (3oz) unsalted roasted
peanuts, chopped

4 tbsp shredded greens

pinch of chilli powder

salt

VARIATIONS

● Use soya milk instead of coconut milk.

● Add 1 red onion, finely sliced and fried, with the beansprouts.

● Use 115g (4oz) brown cap mushrooms instead of beansprouts.

1 Fry the coconut and sugar in a wok or large skillet for 3–4 minutes, or until just browned. Drain and set aside.

2 Heat a little oil in the clean wok or frying pan. Beat 2 eggs with 50ml (2fl oz) of coconut milk. Pour into the hot pan and swirl it around to cover the base and sides. Cook for 1 minute.

BEANSPROUTS

3 Put one quarter of the beansprouts on the omelette. Scatter over one quarter of the peanuts, coconut mixture and greens. Sprinkle with a little chilli powder and salt.

4 Loosen the edges of the omelette and trickle a little oil underneath. Cover and cook for 1 minute more. Fold over, transfer to a warm serving plate and keep warm. Repeat for the other three omelettes. Serve immediately.

Vegetable and Tofu Satay

TOFU IS AN IMPORTANT INGREDIENT *in Thai cooking, and provides a rich source of protein in vegetarian dishes.*

INGREDIENTS

3 tbsp vegetable oil

2 fresh red chillies, seeded and thinly sliced

2 garlic cloves, finely chopped

2.5cm (1in) piece of fresh root ginger, grated

3 tbsp light soy sauce

3 tbsp lemon juice

1 tsp brown sugar

salt

115g (4oz) each button mushrooms, red pepper, cubed aubergine and courgettes

300g (10oz) firm tofu, cubed

FOR THE SAUCE

1 onion, chopped

3 garlic cloves, finely chopped

1 tbsp light soy sauce

2 tbsp lemon juice

½ tsp chilli powder

1 tsp each sugar, ground coriander and ground cumin

400ml (14fl oz) can coconut milk

3 tbsp peanut butter

1 Mix the oil, red chillies, 2 garlic cloves, the ginger, 3 tablespoons each of light soy sauce and lemon juice, the sugar and salt in a large, shallow bowl.

2 Thread the vegetables and tofu on to skewers. Add to the bowl and set aside to marinate for 30 minutes.

4 Add to a saucepan with the coconut milk. Cook, stirring, for 3–4 minutes, or until slightly reduced. Stir in the peanut butter and bring to the boil.

3 Meanwhile, process the onion, the remaining garlic, soy sauce and lemon juice, the chilli powder, sugar, ground coriander, cumin and salt in a blender.

5 Grill the skewers, brushing occasionally with the marinade, for 10–15 minutes, or until browned. Serve at once with the peanut sauce.

MUSHROOMS

Fragrant Vegetable Soup

IN THAILAND SOUP STAYS *on the table during the main course, refreshing the palate between mouthfuls of spicier food.*

INGREDIENTS

50g (2oz) firm tofu, finely diced

25g (1oz) fresh root ginger, grated

rind and juice of 2 limes

1 lemon grass stalk, finely chopped

115g (4oz) shelled fresh peas

115g (4oz) carrots, finely shredded

3 tbsp light soy sauce

600ml (1 pint) vegetable stock

salt and pepper

COOK'S TIP

This is best made with a good homemade stock. Stock freezes well and is a useful 'standby' to keep in the freezer.

VARIATIONS

- Use frozen peas instead of fresh and cook for only 2–3 minutes.
- Use fresh coriander instead of lemon grass and be generous with the lime juice.

1 Boil the tofu in 600ml (1 pint) of water for 1 minute. Remove from the heat and leave in the water for 15 minutes. Drain and set aside, reserving the water.

2 Add the ginger and lime rind to the tofu water and simmer for 15 minutes. Discard the ginger and lime rind.

FRAGRANT VEGETABLE SOUP

3 Add the lemon grass, peas and carrots to the water and return to the boil. Cover and simmer for 5–6 minutes, or until the vegetables are almost cooked.

4 Add the lime juice, tofu, soy sauce and stock. Bring to the boil and simmer for a further 6–7 minutes. Season, if necessary.

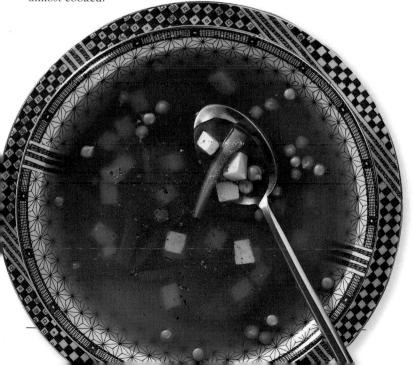

Hot and Sour Soup

WARM AND SATISFYING, *this classic South-east Asian soup is an exquisite accompaniment to a traditional Thai meal.*

INGREDIENTS

900ml (1½ pints) vegetable stock

4 dried Chinese mushrooms, soaked in cold water for 1 hour, drained

115g (4oz) rice vermicelli noodles, soaked and drained

2 lemon grass stalks

4 kaffir lime leaves

115g (4oz) bamboo shoots, sliced

6 tbsp light soy sauce

juice of 1 lime

1 tbsp palm sugar

1 tsp cornflour

4 small fresh green chillies, seeded and finely chopped

6 tbsp rice vinegar

coriander leaves and finely sliced spring onion, to garnish

1 Bring the stock to the boil in a large saucepan. Add the mushrooms, noodles, lemon grass, lime leaves, bamboo shoots, soy sauce, lime juice and sugar. Return to the boil.

VARIATIONS

● Use cider vinegar instead of rice vinegar.

● Use fresh shiitake mushrooms, if available

COOK'S TIP

Bamboo shoots are one of the few Asian vegetables that are canned and widely available.

DRIED MUSHROOMS

2 Mix the cornflour with a little water and stir into the soup. Simmer for 2 minutes, or until slightly thickened.

3 Stir in the chillies and vinegar. Pour into a warmed soup tureen and garnish with coriander and spring onion.

Vegetable Stir-fry with Tamarind

THIS ENTICING DISH OF CRUNCHY *and flavour-packed vegetables is quick and easy to prepare and cook.*

INGREDIENTS

2 garlic cloves, finely chopped

2 small fresh green chillies, seeded and finely chopped

2.5cm (1in) piece of fresh root ginger, grated

2 tbsp vegetable oil

2 small red onions, quartered

175g (6oz) broccoli florets, stems peeled

2 small green peppers, roughly chopped

175g (6oz) spinach, roughly chopped

115g (4oz) sugar snap peas

1 tbsp dark soy sauce

1 tsp sugar

1–2 tbsp tamarind purée

3 tbsp peanut butter

salt and pepper

VARIATIONS

- Use watercress instead of spinach.
- Use mangetout instead of sugar snap peas.
- Use lemon or lime juice instead of tamarind.

1 Gently fry the garlic, chillies and ginger in the vegetable oil in a wok or large frying pan for 1 minute, or until beginning to brown.

2 Add the onions and fry for 2 minutes. Stir in the broccoli and peppers, fry for a further 2 minutes, then add the spinach and fry for another 2 minutes. Finally, add the sugar snap peas and fry for a further 2 minutes.

3 Stir the soy sauce, sugar, tamarind purée and peanut butter into the vegetables.

4 Add 120ml (4fl oz) water to make a sauce and simmer gently, stirring, for a few minutes more. Season and serve immediately.

Green Vegetable Curry

GREEN CURRIES ARE THE HOTTEST *Thai curries and should be made using fresh green chillies.*

INGREDIENTS

175ml (6fl oz) water

grated rind of 1 lime

1 green pepper, seeded and chopped

4 fresh green chillies, seeded and chopped

1 lemon grass stalk, chopped

1 bunch of watercress

2 tbsp chopped coriander

4 spinach leaves

3 garlic cloves

5cm (2in) piece of fresh root ginger

1 tsp each ground coriander and cumin

4 tbsp vegetable oil

2 tbsp desiccated coconut

175g (6oz) baby sweetcorn

175g (6oz) bamboo shoots

4 kaffir lime leaves, torn

115g (4oz) canned water chestnuts, halved (reserve some liquid)

salt and ground white pepper

basil sprigs and lime wedges, to garnish

VARIATIONS

● Use red chillies instead of green chillies.

● Use lemon rind and wedges instead of lime.

● Add 5 coriander roots to the chilli paste.

1 Boil the water and lime rind for 1 minute. Leave to cool.

2 Purée the pepper, chillies, lemon grass, watercress, chopped coriander, spinach, garlic, ginger, ground coriander, cumin and seasoning. If necessary, add a little water to keep the purée smooth. Stir-fry in the oil in a wok or large frying pan for 5 minutes.

LEMON GRASS

3 Strain the lime water and mix with the coconut to produce a fairly runny paste. Stir into the pan.

4 Add the sweetcorn, bamboo shoots, kaffir lime leaves and water chestnuts with a little of their liquid. Simmer for about 10 minutes. Serve garnished with basil and lime.

Sweet Potato Curry

This curry has an inviting fragrance. The coconut milk separates in the can so do not shake it before opening.

INGREDIENTS

2 large dried red chillies, soaked briefly
in warm water

1 shallot, quartered

1 garlic clove, chopped

2.5cm (1in) piece of fresh root ginger,
roughly chopped

6 white peppercorns

pinch each of coriander seeds and
ground cumin

1–2 star anise

1 tsp chopped lemon grass

1 tsp grated lime rind

400ml (14fl oz) can coconut milk

1kg (2lb 2oz) sweet potatoes, chopped

175g (6oz) broccoli florets

115g (4oz) fine green beans

6 kaffir lime leaves, roughly torn

2 tbsp light soy sauce

1 tbsp palm sugar

75g (3oz) roasted cashew nuts,
coarsely chopped

2 small fresh red chillies, finely sliced

handful of fresh basil leaves

1 Drain the red chillies and process to a paste in a blender or food processor. Add the shallot, garlic, ginger, peppercorns, coriander seeds, ground cumin, star anise, lemon grass and lime rind and process again. Spoon the top half of the coconut milk into a wok or large frying pan and stir over a medium heat until thickened and reduced by about one half.

2 Add the prepared spice mixture to the pan and cook, stirring, for 3–4 minutes. Stir in the sweet potatoes, broccoli and beans.

VARIATIONS

● Use carrots or parsnips instead of sweet potatoes.

● Use light muscovado or soft brown sugar instead of palm sugar.

● Use peanuts instead of cashew nuts.

3 Mix the remaining coconut milk with 400ml (14fl oz) water and add to the pan with the lime leaves and soy sauce. Cover and simmer for about 10–15 minutes, or until the sweet potatoes are just tender. Stir in the sugar, cashew nuts, fresh chillies and basil.

Tofu with Black Bean Sauce

ALTHOUGH TOFU HAS *a very mild taste, it soaks up the flavours of the other ingredients that are used in a dish.*

INGREDIENTS

250g (9oz) firm tofu, cubed
3 tbsp vegetable oil
3 onions, chopped
3 garlic cloves, finely chopped
1 tsp grated fresh root ginger
1 fresh chilli, finely chopped
2 lemon grass stems
115g (4oz) courgettes, thickly sliced
115g (4oz) mangetout
2 tbsp light soy sauce
2 tbsp black bean sauce
6–8 tbsp water

MANGETOUT

1 Fry the tofu cubes, in batches if necessary, in the vegetable oil in a wok or large frying pan until they turn golden brown. Remove excess oil by draining on kitchen paper, then set aside.

VARIATIONS

● Add sliced carrots to the other vegetables.

● Use sugar snap peas instead of mangetout.

TOFU WITH BLACK BEAN SAUCE

2 Fry the onions, garlic, ginger, chilli and lemon grass for 1 minute.

3 Add the courgettes and mangetout, stir well and fry for 2–3 minutes.

4 Stir in the soy sauce and black bean sauce, return the tofu to the pan and then add 6 tablespoons water. Simmer for 15–20 minutes, or until all the vegetables are just tender; add more water if the vegetables become dry. Be careful not to overcook them. Discard the lemon grass.

COOK'S TIP

For the best flavour, soak the lemon grass stalks in a little warm water for 30 minutes before using.

Thai Fried Noodles

KNOWN AS PAD THAI, *this has almost become the national dish and is one of the best-known Thai dishes worldwide.*

INGREDIENTS

2 garlic cloves, finely chopped

2 tbsp vegetable oil

175g (6oz) thin, flat rice noodles, soaked in boiling water for 20 minutes and drained

1 large egg

2 tbsp lemon juice

2 tbsp dark soy sauce

75g (3oz) firm tofu, diced

1 tbsp chopped preserved radish

75g (3oz) beansprouts

3 spring onions, chopped

1 tbsp chopped coriander

lemon wedges, to garnish

VARIATIONS

● Use lime juice instead of lemon juice.

● Use lime wedges instead of lemon wedges.

1 Fry the garlic in the oil in a wok or large frying pan until just turning golden.

2 Add the noodles and fry gently and briefly. Push to the sides of the pan, add the egg and stir for 2–3 seconds. Stir the noodles and egg together, ensuring that they are thoroughly mixed.

COOK'S TIP

Pickled radish adds a delicious bite to this dish and is available from specialist food stores. Alternatives are pickled cabbage, garlic and other vegetables.

3 Taking each one in turn and stirring quickly after each addition, add the lemon juice, soy sauce, tofu, preserved radish, beansprouts, spring onions and chopped coriander. Work quickly because the total cooking time should not be longer than 3–4 minutes. Serve the pad immediately, garnished with lemon wedges and spring onions.

CORIANDER

Savoury Rice

FRAGRANT, JASMINE RICE *is highly revered in Thailand and is traditionally offered to the gods in the temples.*

INGREDIENTS

1 onion, finely sliced

2 tbsp vegetable oil

450g (1lb) jasmine rice, soaked for
1 hour and drained

1 tsp ground turmeric

1 tsp ground coriander

½ tsp ground cumin

600ml (1 pint) coconut milk

1 cinnamon stick

2 cloves

salt

1 kaffir lime leaf, torn

RICE

COOK'S TIP

Jasmine rice is now widely available. Soaking it before cooking prevents it from sticking as it cooks.

1 Fry the onion in the oil in a wok or large saucepan, stirring, for 2 minutes.

2 Add the rice, turmeric, coriander and cumin and fry for 2 minutes more.

3 Stir in the coconut milk, cinnamon stick, cloves, salt and lime leaf. Bring to the boil, cover the pan and simmer over a low heat for 10 minutes.

4 Discard the cinnamon stick, cloves and lime leaf. Transfer the rice to a warm serving dish and serve to accompany a main course.

VARIATIONS

● Use basmati or patna rice instead of jasmine rice.

● Use vegetable stock instead of coconut milk.

● Use a bay leaf instead of a kaffir lime leaf.

Fried Rice and Beans

THIS IS NOT ONLY *a wholesome and comforting supper dish, but also a highly nutritious one.*

INGREDIENTS

2 garlic cloves, crushed

2 tbsp vegetable oil

1–2 fresh green chillies, seeded and finely chopped

225g (8oz) button mushrooms

6 tbsp cooked or canned haricot beans

1–2 carrots, cut into short strips

2 tomatoes, diced

2 tbsp fresh or canned pineapple chunks (optional)

2 tbsp light soy sauce

1 tsp sugar

½ tsp ground white pepper

75g (3oz) cashew nuts, chopped

225g (8oz) cooked jasmine rice

chopped coriander leaves, to garnish

1 Fry the garlic in the the oil in a large frying pan or wok for 1 minute, or until just turning brown. Add the chillies and fry for a further 30 seconds.

VARIATION

Use strips of courgette in place of carrots.

CORIANDER

2 Add the mushrooms and fry, stirring, for 1 minute, then add the haricot beans, carrots, tomatoes and pineapple (if using) in turn, stirring after each addition. Add the soy sauce, sugar and pepper and stir again.

3 Stir in the nuts and rice and heat until the rice is hot. Transfer to a warm serving dish and garnish with chopped coriander leaves.

COOK'S TIP

For 225g (8oz) cooked rice you will need about 65g (2½oz) raw rice.

Shiitake Mushroom Kebabs with Dipping Sauce

THESE MUSHROOMS WILL *taste even better if they are cooked, Thai-style – over a barbecue or charcoal fire.*

INGREDIENTS

FOR THE KEBABS

115g (4oz) dried shiitake mushrooms, soaked for 1 hour and drained

4 large garlic cloves, crushed

1 tsp ground black pepper

1 tsp ground coriander

1 tbsp sugar

1 tbsp light soy sauce

FOR THE SAUCE

1 tbsp sugar

5 tbsp rice vinegar

salt

3–4 small fresh red chillies, seeded and finely chopped

VARIATIONS

- Use green chillies in place of red chillies.

- Use cider vinegar instead of rice vinegar.

1 Pat the mushrooms dry with kitchen paper and put in a bowl.

SHIITAKE MUSHROOM KEBABS WITH DIPPING SAUCE

2 Mix three-quarters of the garlic, the black pepper, coriander, half the sugar and the soy sauce together in a small bowl. Pour over the mushrooms and marinate for at least 30 minutes.

4 Thread the mushrooms on to bamboo skewers and cook under a preheated grill for about 1 minute on each side, or until sizzling. Serve immediately with a separate bowl of sauce for each plate.

RED CHILLIES

3 To make the sweet-sour dipping sauce, gradually bring the remaining sugar, the rice vinegar and salt to a simmer in a small pan. Leave the sauce to cool, then stir in the remaining garlic and the chopped red chillies.

COOK'S TIP

Soak the bamboo skewers in cold water for 30 minutes before threading them to make sure that they do not burn when they are grilled.

Savoury Fruit Salad

THIS COMBINATION OF *sweet fruit and refreshing, slightly sour salad dressing is a most successful dish.*

INGREDIENTS

FOR THE SAUCE

6 tbsp sunflower oil

1 tbsp each lemon juice, soy sauce and finely chopped lemon grass

1 tsp brown sugar

1 fresh green chilli, seeded and finely chopped

1 garlic clove, finely chopped

FOR THE SALAD

2 tbsp chopped basil

1 tbsp finely chopped coriander

8 each orange, grapefruit and lime segments

12 strawberries, quartered

16 raspberries

flesh of 1 small honeydew melon, chopped

175g (6oz) water melon flesh, chopped

16 seedless white grapes, halved

crisp lettuce leaves, to serve

mint sprigs, and 4 spring onions, green part only, chopped, to garnish

STRAWBERRIES

1 To make the dressing, mix together the oil, lemon juice, soy sauce, lemon grass, sugar, chilli and garlic. Cover and chill.

BASIL

VARIATIONS

● Add sliced tart green apples.

● Add pineapple chunks and sliced bananas.

● Use rice vinegar instead of lemon juice.

2 Just before serving, mix the herbs and fruit with the dressing in a large bowl.

COOK'S TIP

Make sure the dressing is really chilled before making the fruit salad.

3 Arrange the lettuce leaves on a serving platter or individual serving plates and pile the fruit on top. Garnish with mint sprigs and chopped spring onions.

Banana Fritters

THESE ARE SOLD IN *Thailand as a snack on street corners. In the West, they can be served as a snack or for dessert.*

INGREDIENTS

3 tbsp rice flour

3 tbsp cornflour

1 egg, beaten

4 ripe but firm bananas

oil for deep-frying

caster sugar, for dusting

lime wedges, to serve

BANANA

1 Sift the rice flour and cornflour into a mixing bowl. Make a well in the centre and add the egg. Stir together, adding about 4 tablespoons water, to form a smooth batter. The batter should be pourable, but still thick enough to coat the pieces of banana.

VARIATIONS

● Use apples instead of bananas.

● Use lemon rather than lime.

● Use a half-and-half mixture of water and coconut milk, rather than water alone.

LIME SLICES

2 Peel the bananas and slice widthways into chunks.

3 Dip the banana pieces in the batter. Add a few pieces to hot oil in a deep-fat frying pan. Fry for 3–4 minutes, or until golden brown and crisp. Drain off excess oil on kitchen paper. Dust with sugar and serve with lime wedges.

Sticky Rice Cakes

THESE SWEET CAKES CAN BE SERVED *as a snack or as a dessert and are delicious with Coconut Milk Pudding or tropical fruit.*

INGREDIENTS

225g (8oz) sticky rice

120ml (4fl oz) coconut milk

150g (5oz) palm sugar

2 tbsp roasted sesame seeds

VARIATION

Use light muscovado sugar or soft brown sugar instead of palm sugar.

1 Soak the rice in boiling water for 2 hours. Drain, then steam for 30–35 minutes, or until tender. Spread the rice out well on a plate and leave to cool for a minimum of 2 hours.

2 Cook the coconut milk and palm sugar in a large, preferably non-stick, frying pan over a medium heat, stirring occasionally, for about 20–30 minutes, or until the mixture thickens and becomes slightly caramelized.

3 Lower the heat. Add the rice and stir thoroughly into the milk, then remove the pan from the heat.

4 Spread the rice evenly in an oiled 20cm (8in) cake tin. Scatter over the sesame seeds. Leave until cold, then cut into small squares.

PALM SUGAR

COOK'S TIP

Do not refrigerate the rice cakes; they will keep perfectly for 24 hours. After that, cover the cakes and put them in a cool place, where they will keep fresh for several days.

Coconut Milk Pudding

THIS SIMPLE STEAMED COCONUT CUSTARD *makes a refreshing end to a spicy Thai meal.*

INGREDIENTS

250ml (8fl oz) coconut milk

3 tbsp palm sugar

4 large eggs

Desiccated coconut, to decorate

EGGS

COOK'S TIP

This dish may also be cooked in the oven. Divide the custard between individual ramekins and stand them in a roasting tin half-filled with hot water. Bake in a preheated oven at 150°C/300°F/Gas 2 for 35–40 minutes.

1 Stir the coconut milk with the sugar until the sugar has dissolved. Beat in the eggs, one at a time, until they are fully incorporated.

2 Pour the coconut custard into a 20cm (8in) ovenproof dish or cake tin about 5cm (2in) deep.

VARIATIONS

● Use light muscovado sugar or soft brown sugar instead of palm sugar.

● Use ducks' eggs instead of hens' eggs.

3 Put the dish in the top half of a steamer, cover and steam for 25–30 minutes, or until a skewer or fork inserted into the centre comes out clean. Leave to cool.

COCONUT

Crisp Basil Leaves

A GARNISH OF CRISP BASIL *leaves make all the difference to the flavour and appearance of any dish.*

INGREDIENTS

vegetable oil, for deep-frying

leaves from 25g (1oz) basil sprigs

VARIATIONS

● Use mint leaves instead of basil.

● Add a finely chopped red chilli to the oil.

1 Heat the oil in a wok or deep-fat frying pan until very hot, but not smoking. Add the basil leaves, in batches, and fry for 1 minute, by which time they should be crisp.

2 Remove the basil leaves from the pan with a slotted spoon and drain thoroughly on absorbent kitchen paper before using.

3 Continue in this way until all the basil leaves have been used.

Further reading

30 Minute Thai Cookbook, *Sarah Beattie* (Thorsons, 1997)

Vegetarian Thai Cooking, *Cara Hobday*, (Parragon, 1995)

Thai Vegetarian Cooking, *Vatcharin Bhumichtir* (Pavilion, 1992)

Vegetarian Thai, *Jackum Brown* (Hamlyn, 1998)

The Vegetarian Table: Thailand, *Jacki Passmore* (Chronicle Books, 1997)

Real Thai Vegetarian, *Nancie McDermott* (Chronicle Books, 1997)

Step by Step Vegetarian Thai (Parragon, 1997)

Useful addresses

The Vegetarian Society
Parkdale
Durham Road
Altrincham
Cheshire WA14 4QG
UK

**The Vegetarian Union
of North America**
PO Box 9710
Washington DC 20016
USA

**The Australian
Vegetarian Society**
PO Box 65
2021 Paddington
Australia

The Soil Association
86 Colston Street
Bristol BS1 5BB
UK

Farm Verified Organic
RR 1
Box 40A USA
Medina
ND 58467
USA

**National Association for
Sustainable Agriculture**
PO Box 768
AUS-Sterling
SA 5152
Australia